♡From:

....

♡To:

....

....

....

....

Your words are my motivation, and your life success **stories** are my guiding light. I love you, dear mother. **Thank you** For your love, care, and support.

Thank you for getting your copy of our book.
If you like this book and find it useful,
we would be grateful if you share your review with us.

This keepsake book is intended to be given to your mother as a gift, encouraging her to write down stories, memories, experiences, thoughts, and feelings, guided by thoughtful prompts.

You can find some questions that you'd rather not answer or that aren't practical, and you can replace them with more appropriate ones.

Fill in the Book, draw, sketch, doodle, and stick some pictures in the pages, then return it to your children so they can keep and share your memories as well.

When and where were you born?
What do you still remember about
the place where you grew up?

....

....

....

....

....

....

....

....

....

....

....

....

What were the names of your parents/grandparents, and what did they look like?

....

....

....

....

....

....

....

....

....

....

....

....

....

What kind of work did your parents\grandparents do?

....

....

....

....

....

....

....

....

....

....

....

....

....

Tell me about your brothers and sisters.

....

....

....

....

....

....

....

....

....

....

....

....

What do you remember about your grandparents?

....

....

....

....

....

....

....

....

....

....

....

....

Have you ever been punished by your parents for having a bad habit?

Who was stringent, your mother or your father?

....

....

....

....

....

....

....

....

....

....

....

....

What was your house like when you were a child?

....

....

....

....

....

....

....

....

....

....

....

....

What kind of games were popular when you were a kid?

_____

_____

_____

_____

_____

_____

_____

_____

_____

_____

_____

_____

Who were the best friends of your childhood? And how did you pass your time together? DO YOU REMAIN IN CONTACT WITH ANY OF YOUR CHILDHOOD FRIENDS? Who are your closest friends to this day?

....

....

....

....

....

....

....

....

....

....

....

....

Did you have a nickname when you were growing up?

....

....

....

....

....

....

....

....

....

....

....

....

What was your school like? Did you enjoy going to school? What do you remember about your favorite teacher?

_____

_____

_____

_____

_____

_____

_____

_____

_____

_____

_____

_____

Did you go to college or get additional training after high school? What did you study? At what age have you finished school?

....

....

....

....

....

....

....

....

....

....

....

....

....

What were you always good at?

....

....

....

....

....

....

....

....

....

....

....

....

What kind of things scared you as a child?

When you grew up, What was your favorite holidays, and how did you celebrate them?

....

....

....

....

....

....

....

....

....

....

....

....

How did you celebrate your birthdays?

....

....

....

....

....

....

....

....

....

....

....

....

What's the best
Christmas/birthday gift you've
ever had?

....

....

....

....

....

....

....

....

....

....

....

....

Have you got an allowance? How much was that, and what did you spend your money on?

_____

_____

_____

_____

_____

_____

_____

_____

_____

_____

_____

_____

What did you want to become when you were young?

....

....

....

....

....

....

....

....

....

....

....

....

Have you ever had a pet? What was it? And what was its name?

_____

_____

_____

_____

_____

_____

_____

_____

_____

_____

_____

_____

How was your relationship with your own parents? In childhood, in your teenage years, in adulthood? Do you see any differences between yours and our own relationship? If so, then what?

What are your favorite childhood memories?

What made you the most nervous in your adolescent years?

....

....

....

....

....

....

....

....

....

....

....

....

What was the happiest/saddest moment you had as a teenager?

....

....

....

....

....

....

....

....

....

....

....

....

....

What were your favorite hobbies when you grew up?

....

....

....

....

....

....

....

....

....

....

....

....

....

Tell me about the time you learned to drive a vehicle. What was your first car?

....

....

....

....

....

....

....

....

....

....

....

....

Describe your first work ?What was your profession ? and how did you choose it? How many jobs have you had?

....

....

....

....

....

....

....

....

....

....

....

....

....

....

What kind of thing did you like to spend money on?

....

....

....

....

....

....

....

....

....

....

....

....

....

Tell me about your first house.

Who was your first love? Do you believe in love at first sight?

....

....

....

....

....

....

....

....

....

....

....

....

....

Did you ever have your heart broken?

....

....

....

....

....

....

....

....

....

....

....

....

....

How did you meet my father? How did he ask you to marry him? and what was your wedding like? Where did you go for honeymoon?

....

....

....

....

....

....

....

....

....

....

....

....

Tell me about the key to a successful marriage.

....

....

....

....

....

....

....

....

....

....

....

....

....

What was your best travel destination?
How many countries have you traveled
to so far? Is there a city or country
that you still want to visit?

....

....

....

....

....

....

....

....

....

....

....

....

Do you have a favorite family vacation memories?

....

....

....

....

....

....

....

....

....

....

....

....

....

Tell me the day your first baby was born.

....

....

....

....

....

....

....

....

....

....

....

....

Were you ever scared to be a parent? What was the first year of motherhood like for you?

_____

_____

_____

_____

_____

_____

_____

_____

_____

_____

_____

_____

Have you been a strict mom?

....

....

....

....

....

....

....

Who helped you take care of me the most often?

....

....

....

....

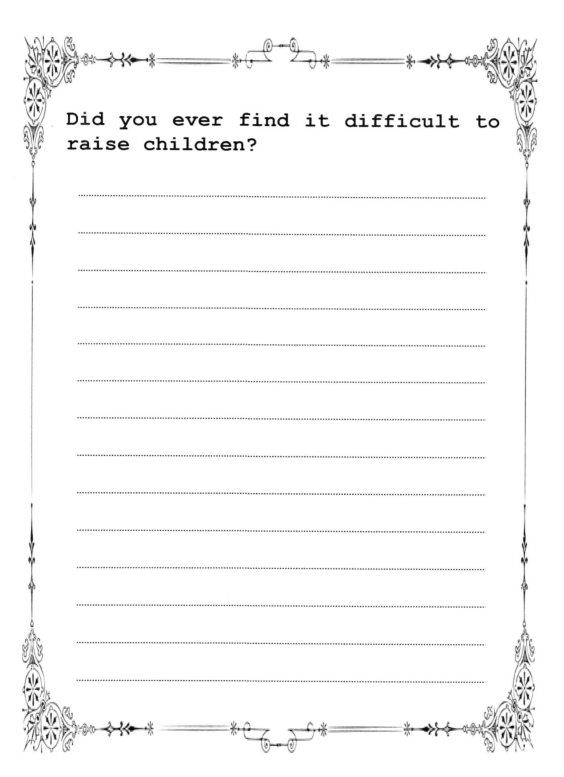

Did you ever find it difficult to raise children?

When I was a baby, did I look more like you or like my father?

....

....

....

....

What was the moment I frustrated you most when I was growing up?

....

....

....

....

....

....

....

What was the moment I hurt you
the most when I grew up?

....

....

....

....

....

....

What is the funniest thing I ever
said or did as a kid?

....

....

....

....

....

What are your favorite memories with me/us?

....

....

....

....

....

....

....

....

....

....

....

....

....

What makes growing up different today than when you were a kid?

....

....

....

....

....

....

....

....

....

....

....

....

What do you wish for me/us ?

....

....

....

....

....

....

....

....

....

....

....

....

....

How do you advise your younger self when you are 20? 30? 40?

....

....

....

....

....

....

....

....

....

....

....

....

Select three words to describe your personality.

....

....

....

....

....

....

....

....

....

....

....

....

Has anyone ever disappointed you?

What is your spiritual background? Are you a religious practicing? How did religion affect your life?

....

....

....

....

....

....

....

....

....

....

....

....

What or who is your favorite:

Artist	
Athlete	
Author	
Singer	
Musical group	
Book	
Painting	
Movie	
Songs	
Musical Instrument	
TV show	
Season	
Restaurant	
Color	
Animal	

Do you play any musical instrument? If yes, which one? And what can you tell about its basics?

Did you play any sports?

....

....

....

....

....

....

....

What is your favorite sports team?

....

....

....

....

Do you like cooking ? Do you still
remember your first cooked dish?
What is your favorite dishes ?what
is your disliked one ?

....
....
....
....
....
....
....
....
....
....
....
....

Were any recipes passed down from family members to you? Could you give me one of the best?

....

....

....

....

....

....

....

....

....

....

....

....

....

Recipe: ....

Ingredients:

....

....

....

....

....

Instructions:

....

....

....

....

....

....

Notes:

....

....

....

....

....

....

Place a photo of
your recipe here

Which activities are you currently enjoying?

_____

_____

_____

_____

_____

_____

_____

_____

_____

_____

_____

_____

_____

Where is your place to go to relax?

_____

_____

_____

_____

_____

_____

_____

_____

_____

_____

_____

_____

What makes you happy?

Tell me about one of the happiest
memories you have.

Do you believe that money can buy
happiness? And why or why not?

_____

_____

_____

_____

_____

_____

_____

_____

_____

_____

_____

_____

_____

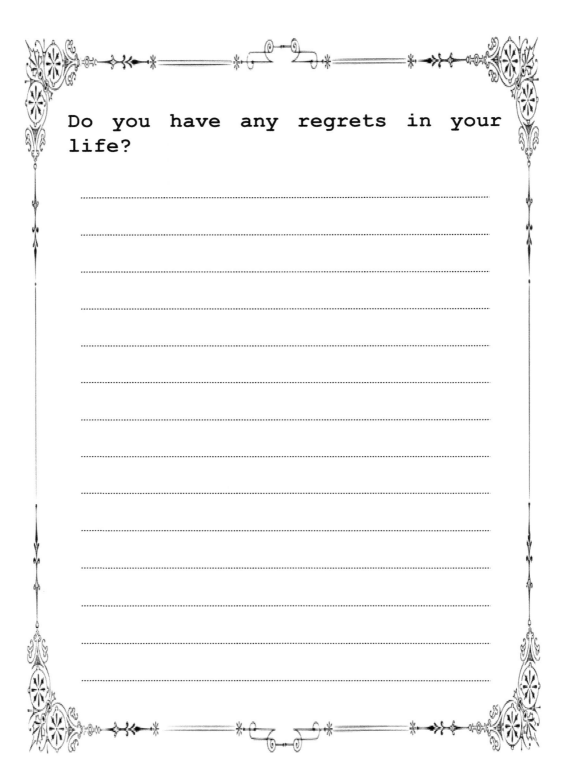

Do you have any regrets in your life?

What is your best decision ever?

....

....

....

....

....

....

....

....

....

....

....

....

If you could go back to any age, what would it be? And why?

....
....
....
....
....
....
....
....
....
....
....
....

How have your dreams and goals changed across your life?

If you could go back in time to choose a new career for yourself, would you? What would you choose to do?

....

....

....

....

....

....

....

....

....

....

....

What important lessons did you learn in your life?

Tell me things you are most proud of.

....

....

....

....

....

....

....

....

....

....

....

....

What is something you still want to learn?

How do you treat stress?

....
....
....
....
....
....
....
....
....
....
....
....
....
....

What are you grateful for?

What is your favorite invention of technology that has happened in your lifetime?

If you could take three things on a desert island, what objects would you select?

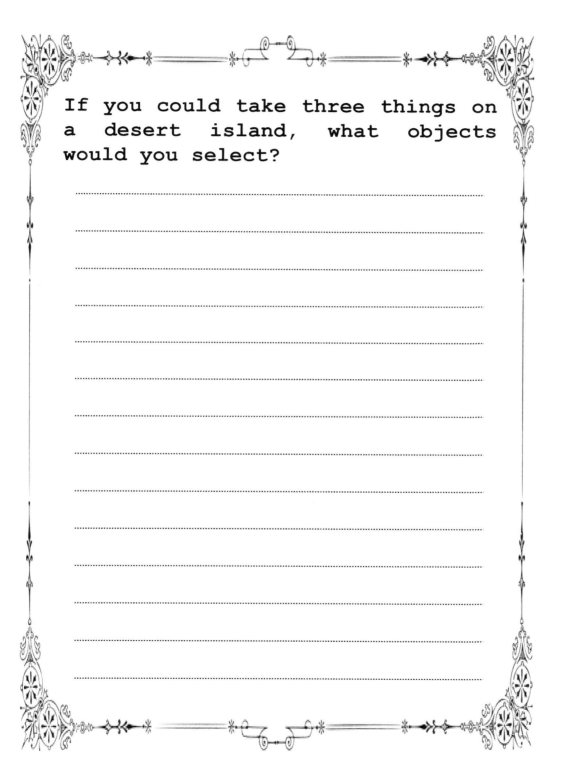

If you could have only one food
to eat at every meal each day,
what would it be?

If you were allowed to live in
another place, where would it be?
Why then?

_____

_____

_____

_____

_____

_____

_____

_____

_____

_____

_____

_____

If there were one superpower you could have, what would it be and why?

_____

_____

_____

_____

_____

_____

_____

_____

_____

_____

_____

_____

_____

What are some things most people don't know about you?

....

....

....

....

....

....

....

....

....

....

....

....

What do you want your great- and great-great-grandchildren to know about you?

....

....

....

....

....

....

....

....

....

....

....

....

What are your goals for the future?

_____

_____

_____

_____

_____

_____

_____

_____

_____

_____

_____

_____

What traditions do you most want our family to continue?

....
....
....
....
....
....
....
....
....
....
....
....

Do you have any unrealized dreams?

....

....

....

....

....

....

....

....

....

....

....

....

....

....

If there's any piece of advice
that you feel you need to share,
what would it be?

....

....

....

....

....

....

....

....

....

....

....

....

What would your perfect day be like? Describe it

....

....

....

....

....

....

....

....

....

....

....

....

....

Why do you love me?

....

....

....

....

....

....

....

....

....

....

....

....

Do you want to talk about anything else?

....

....

....

....

....

....

....

....

....

....

....

....

....

Do you have any questions for me
that you'd like to ask?

_____

_____

_____

_____

_____

_____

_____

_____

_____

_____

_____

_____

_____

_____

IF YOU HAVE ANY FAMILY PHOTOS,
PLEASE INCLUDE THEM HERE....

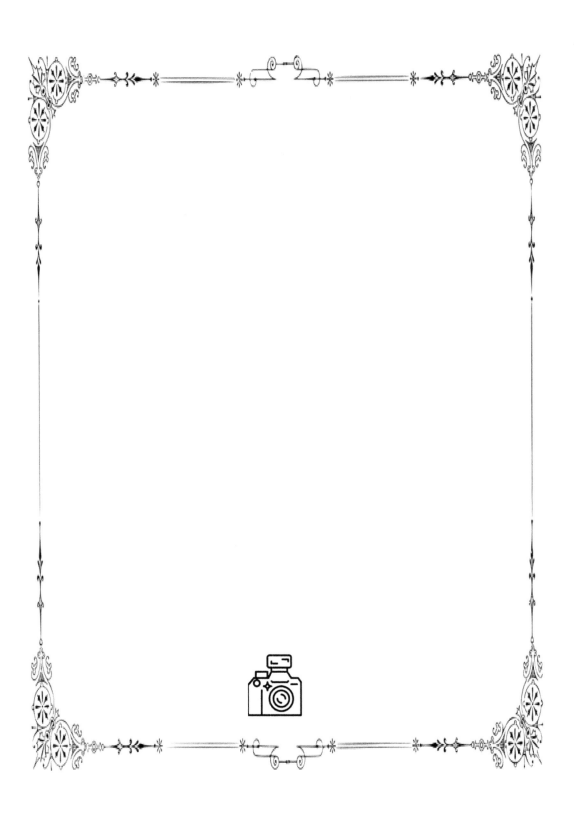

Printed in Great Britain
by Amazon

80434632R00059